COURSE CONCLUSION
BEYOND THE DEBATES?

Prepared for the course team by Maud Blair

The Open University, Walton Hall, Milton Keynes MK7 6AA

First published 1992. Reprinted 1996

Designed by the Graphic Design Group of the Open University

Typeset by the Open University and printed in the United Kingdom by Hobbs the Printers Ltd, Brunel Road, Totton, Hampshire SO40 3WX

ISBN 0 7492 31114

1.2

Cover photograph © Ingrid Pollard

CONTENTS

1   INTRODUCTION

1.1   Aims and objectives

The aims of this Conclusion are three-fold:

- to help you revise the main themes and consolidate your understanding of the key concepts employed in the course;
- to make links across the blocks;
- to discuss the debates around various concepts and reflect on the implications for practice.

There are no TMAs set for this final section of the course, but we hope it will prove particularly helpful when you come to prepare for the examination. For this reason we have set a number of optional activities. These are not meant to take up more than a few minutes of your time, but should be useful as part of your revision.

The main function of this Conclusion is to engage you in an active review of the different ways in which problems are defined and to assess the implications of these different definitions for policy and practice. As you have been studying this course, the debates have been continuing – at national, local and community level; in schools, in 'academia' and in tutorial groups for ED356. People's lives continue to be affected by the policies, practices, decisions and strategies we have been discussing. Our hope is that you, the students, have acquired sufficient understanding of these debates for them to have some meaning in your everyday lives.

What is important to note is the timely nature of this course. The 1990s bring with them enormous local and global political, economic and social changes. There are changed and changing political and economic priorities in Eastern Europe which underline the concerns about identity and 'nation' discussed in Block 2. There is the inexorable move towards the dismantling of the system of apartheid in South Africa and the implications therein for global racial politics, and the end of an historical era in Hong Kong as government is transferred from Britain to China, possibly opening up another phase in the politics of migration to Britain. The re-drawing of economic boundaries around the European Community throws into stark relief questions of belonging and of citizenship for Europe's minority ethnic groups, whilst at the same time raising concerns about global relationships between the rich and poor sections of the world.

1.2   Resources

This concluding part of the course necessarily makes frequent reference to the resources you have already studied. As well as the Course Introduction and the three Study Guides, you will need to keep the three Readers and the Resource Book close to hand:

Reader 1: GILL, D., MAYOR, B. and BLAIR, M. (eds) (1992) *Racism and Education: structures and strategies*, London, Sage/The Open University.

Reader 2: DONALD, J. and RATTANSI, A. (eds) (1992) *'Race', Culture and Difference*, London, Sage/The Open University.

Reader 3: BRAHAM, P., RATTANSI, A. and SKELLINGTON, R. (eds) (1992) *Racism and Antiracism: inequalities, opportunities and policies*, London, Sage/The Open University.

The Resource Book: SKELLINGTON, R. with MORRIS, P. and GORDON, P. (1992) *'Race' in Britain Today*, London, Sage/The Open University.

The Conclusion itself is made up of this text, Audio-cassette 4 and TV8, *Beyond the Debates*.

1.3   Setting the scene

While each of the blocks of this course was structured around a specific focus and drew on particular perspectives, they were not, of course, discrete entities. There are common themes running across them and in discussing these themes we propose to bring together the different perspectives and examine where the differences and similarities lie. As a course team, we too have differed on some of these issues because our interpretations of particular texts have differed. As the author of this Conclusion, I will signal to you in a boxed 'author's comment' when a view is my own and not necessarily representative of the course team as a whole. In the final analysis, my views represent *my* interpretation of the text and may be quite different from *your* interpretation. We hope that at this stage in the course you will not only be familiar with the main themes and concepts, but will also be able to use your skills of analysis and judgement to draw your own conclusions.

The accounts provided in various parts of the course – in particular in the Resource Book and Reader 3 – revealed the extent and the persistence of racism in British society. The course focused on the theoretical and practical aspects of racism and discrimination against black people – the 'visible' minorities. We know, of course, that black people are not the only ones to experience racism, as the Course Introduction set out to show. We would not wish to diminish the seriousness of racism against white minority groups. For example, anti-Semitism has remained a constant theme in the activities of fascist organizations. In TV7, *Young Turks in Germany: Education for What?*, you observed how the opportunities and life chances of Turkish communities in Germany are restricted either by institutional constraints or by the direct actions of fascist groups. We are aware, also, that Travellers and Gypsies experience blatant racism in their struggles for adequate sites and to maintain a distinctive life-style. It might be argued, however, that through an examination of racism against black people it is possible to understand the *processes* which characterize racism and discrimination against other groups. Brah, for example, argues that '... anti-black and anti-Irish racism (for example) situates these groups differently within British society. As white Europeans, the great majority of Irish people are placed in a dominant position *vis-à-vis* black people in and through the discourse of anti-black racism, even when the two groups may share the same class location. In other words we assume different subject positions within various racisms' (Reader 2, p. 133).

1.4   Structure of the Course Conclusion

This Conclusion picks out themes and concepts that are significant either because they run through the whole course, or because they are central to a particular block. These key themes are: analyzing racism; essentialism and reductionism; institutional racism; institutional policy; equal opportunities policies; the education debate; other strategies to counter racism; identity and forms of mobilization. I review the various theoretical assumptions of the contributors to ED356, drawing attention to the differences and similarities where they occur. As far as possible the themes are dealt with in the order listed here, but, as the themes themselves are not mutually exclusive, there are frequent cross references.

Analyzing racism

We will re-visit the general conceptual frameworks used to analyze racism, looking in particular at the concepts of *ideology* and *discourse*.

Essentialism and reductionism

These concepts were specifically discussed in Block 2, but were important to the analysis of racism throughout the course. Through such concepts we can attempt to establish what racism is *not* as opposed to what it *is*. These questions have had an important influence on the politics of the Left in re-conceptualizing categories such as *class*, and on *feminist* methods of analysis.

Institutional racism

Racism, it is suggested, is manifested through both individual actions and the procedures of institutions. I summarize the discussion of the concept and nature of institutional racism presented in Block 3.

Institutional policy

How effective are official policies in the attempts to tackle racism and racial discrimination? This was a central theme in Blocks 1 and 3. I go on to look at the particular case of equal opportunities policies.

The education debate

The concept of cultural diversity was an important theme in Block 2. What are the different understandings of culture? I link this to the discussions in Block 1, and ask how the concept of cultural diversity has been understood within the arena of education, and what implications this has for strategy.

Other strategies to counter racism

I look in particular at the strategies of *racism awareness training*, which were generally related to racism as prejudice, and *antiracist education* which was, again in general terms, a strategy for dealing with racism as ideology. This necessarily entails an examination of the critique of antiracism and the viability of antiracist strategies for tackling racism.

Identity and forms of mobilization

How do groups *mobilize* against exclusion and marginalization and against discrimination? The concept of *difference* is important to this debate. I look at the contentions around the term *'black'* as a symbol of political unity. These questions have also had an important influence on questions of gender and how *women* mobilize. Other forms of exclusion, for example on the basis of disability or sexuality, were not specifically addressed in the course, but I hope that you will have gained sufficient understanding of the forms of analysis and the modes of critique we have applied to racism to be able to apply them to other areas of social interaction.

2   ANALYZING RACISM

2.1   Introduction

In this section I want to take a step back and look at the frameworks
of analysis and the theoretical concepts used by contributors to
ED356. In subsequent sections we will go on to consider particular
analyses and manifestations of racism. First, though, it will be useful
to clarify our intellectual framework, particularly the concepts of
ideology and *discourse*.

2.2   Ideology

Ideology can be generally understood as the means by which people
make sense of their own social reality. Particular ideologies are
embodied in the everyday language, thoughts, ideas, attitudes as well
as actions of groups and help to create and re-create a sense of shared
identity. As such, ideology is a *process* and not a static phenomenon.
Ideology is racist when the notion of 'race' as biological or cultural
inferiority is introduced into a group's *common-sense* understanding
of the world and becomes *routinized* in that group's social relations
with other groups. Racist ideology is elaborated and disseminated
through various means. Some of the major means of dissemination are
through different *structures* of society. These include:

- *government policies*: for example, the definition of 'intentional
  homelessness' in the 1989 Local Government and Housing Act
  which has a discriminatory effect, particularly on Bangladeshi
  families (see Ginsburg, Reader 3);

- *the media*: the articles by Ouseley and Richardson in Reader 1
  outlined the role played by the media in disseminating racist
  ideologies. The power of the media in influencing public opinion
  was an important site of contestation in the General Election of
  April 1992;

- *statutory services*: education, discussed in Block 1, is a particularly
  important source of ideological dissemination. Hardy and Vieler-
  Porter (Reader 1) argue this point in relation to the Education
  Reform Act. Other services, such as the police and the social
  services, discussed in Block 3, function on the basis of certain
  assumptions and therefore promote particular versions of society;

- *academic works*: these, too, influence social thinking and social policy in specific ways. (For example, Eysenck's ideas on intelligence and their impact on education.)

It could be argued, therefore, that racism is a *structural* phenomenon.

On Audio-cassette 1 Stuart Hall referred to 'race' as a 'terrain'. 'Race' can be considered the terrain upon which *racialized* relations are produced and reproduced. Racist ideology is, therefore, subject to continuous change and takes different shapes and forms according to the specific conditions of a particular place and time. In colonial times, for example, racist ideologies which constructed the white subject as biologically and culturally superior were created and reproduced for the purpose of maintaining political and economic control over colonized peoples. You saw, in the article by Gauri Viswanathan in Reader 2, how 'literature' was one strategy used for this purpose. In contemporary Britain, the terrain has shifted from the idea of biological inferiority to that of *cultural difference*. Stuart Hall argues in 'New ethnicities' that:

> ethnicity, in the form of a culturally constructed sense of Englishness and a particularly closed, exclusive and regressive form of English national identity, is one of the core characteristics of British racism today.
>
> (Reader 2, p. 256)

Racist ideology creates exclusive forms of representation, rendering the racialized group 'outsiders' and, by implication, inferior. This is particularly evident in the literature on immigration and the labour market and racial harassment and violence. John Solomos (Reader 3) shows how definitions of black immigration were linked not only to 'race' relations, but to specific definitions of 'Britishness' which excluded people on the grounds of skin colour, simultaneously rendering them 'alien' and a threat.

2.3   Discourse

Having studied ED356, you will now be thoroughly familiar with the term 'discourse'. Turn now to page 40 of the Course Introduction and look again at the full definition of discourse provided there.

Activity 1

You may still be feeling a little confused about the distinction between *ideology* and *discourse*. There is no doubt that the relation between them can be confusing. Should you wish clarify your understanding, ten or fifteen minutes spent considering the following questions should help. The comment that follows will, I hope, help further.

- In which ways might the definition of ideology given in Section 2.2 differ from the definition of discourse in the Course Introduction?
- Are the two terms mutually exclusive?
- Do the differences reflect different theoretical positions?

Comment

The distinction between ideology and discourse is not clear-cut. Confusion arises partly because both terms are used in a variety of ways, so that it is not always clear if we are comparing like with like. 'Discourse' can be hard to pin down because it is central to new and emergent intellectual developments.

However, a clear-cut distinction between ideology and discourse *is* made in Study Guide 2. This arises from a specific view expressed in that study guide that antiracists consider ideology to be *a set of fixed ideas* and racism to be *a form of false consciousness*. For example, you were asked to compare the article by Kenneth Parker in Reader 1 with that by Gauri Viswanathan in Reader 2, as exemplifying the difference between an analysis that uses the concept of ideology as a framework and one that uses discourse. You might like to consider the alternative view that both writers are concerned with how literature is used as a mechanism of ideological reproduction, in one instance to control a colonial population, and in the other to maintain the myth of an exclusive English literary canon, thus inferiorizing and excluding 'Other' forms of literature. Viswanathan, for example, confirms Parker's view when she states:

> My argument is that literary study gained enormous cultural strength through its development in a period of territorial expansion and conquest, and that *the subsequent institutionalization of the discipline in England itself took on a shape and an ideological content developed in the colonial context.*
> (Reader 2, p. 149, *my emphasis*)

Thus, I am not convinced that the Parker and Viswanathan articles exemplify different analyses of racism, or, indeed, that the concepts of ideology and discourse are mutually exclusive.

If we accept that ideology, in general, is 'the means by which people make sense of their own social reality' (Section 2.2), the concept of discourse can be subsumed under this general framework of ideology. 'Discourse analysis' would thus be a particular approach to the intellectual reproduction of ideas, an approach characterized by an overriding concern with the fact that language does not provide 'a neutral medium in which to describe objects' (Course Introduction, p. 40).

As an analytic approach, discourse analysis tends to concentrate on the realm of language, since 'discourse introduces the idea that it is through language, categories and concepts that we bring objects into being' (ibid.). This definition of discourse suggests a philosophically idealist position in that it denies any reliable access to objective reality.

The concept of ideology, on the other hand, does not necessarily preclude a belief in the validity of empirical evidence and thus allows for some purchase on the material manifestations of racism.

3 ESSENTIALISM AND REDUCTIONISM

The terms 'essentialism' and 'reductionism' describe a tendency to isolate single causes and ignore dynamic and dialectical processes and multiple causation. A theme that runs through this course is the necessity for rigorous understanding of the different ways in which racism is manifested. The danger of reducing black people's experiences wholly to racism, it has been pointed out, can obscure other underlying or interlinking explanations for discrimination. Contributors to ED356 have criticized strategies based on the assumption that human beings are straightforward and uncomplicated and that overlook ambiguities and contradictions in the subjective self.

The definition of racism as combining prejudice with power, for example, was the basis of specific forms of antiracist strategy which predominated in the late 1970s and early 1980s. The assumption was that white people were prejudiced against black people and had the power to express their prejudices in concrete ways to prevent black people from benefiting equally from the nation's resources. This was expressed in the formula: *prejudice + power = racism*. This definition of racism posited racism in *prejudiced individuals*. An essentialist view of racism would, therefore, see racism as *personified* in (dominant) white groups, as in the example of prejudice and power given above. Whilst it might be argued that this may indeed be a component in an understanding of racism, it is obviously inadequate to explain the contradictions and ambiguities of racism.

Another way to view racism is to examine not what it *is*, but what it is *not*. Rattansi and Cohen (Reader 2) stress that racism cannot be defined in terms of a fixed content (like a stick of rock), or 'passed on' (like a disease). Neither is it primarily or necessarily a matter of beliefs. (The contradictory relations of white teachers with black students in Wright's study in Reader 1 confirm this.) Nor of attitudes, as John Wrench's study of the careers service in Reader 3 shows. Beliefs and attitudes may be part of the explanation for different policies or different actions, but they are not sufficient explanations.

It is not that 'race' *is*, or that black people *are* such and such which leads to their being discriminated against, as clearly black people, like white people, are a diverse collection. Rather, it is the way that black people as a group are ideologically constructed, with 'race' (often in the guise of ethnicity) as the framework, which might help to explain the different and changing forms and the effects and tenacity of racism. The reasons for this construction may be varied – to preserve particular houses for whites, to exclude black people from competing for jobs, to restrict entry into a country, and so on. The modes of dissemination may be through individuals but they would also include the structures and various institutions of society. At the same time, the less powerful groups do not merely internalize negative representations and constructions of themselves, but resist and struggle to change these representations and create alternative ways of making sense of reality.

Cohen (Reader 2) and Troyna and Hatcher (Reader 1), in studies of racism amongst white youth and school children, point to the gender, class, generational and environmental dimensions of young white people's attitudes and behaviours. They suggest that an exclusive focus on the racism of these young people in, for example, attempts to deal with racist harassment, could deny the opportunity to develop more refined strategies and risk the possibility of racist views becoming even more attractive. Bagley (Reader 1) also contends that it is necessary to consider the (often unintended) racially discriminatory actions of teachers in the context of wider ideologies of teacher *professionalism*. Although racism encircles black people in many areas of their lives, it is not the only factor which needs to be considered, a point to which black women in particular have long testified and which has been underlined by various contributors to this course.

Similar anti-essentialist and anti-reductionist arguments were made in Study Guide 3. In relation to institutional racism in the allocation of council housing and in the social services, for example, it was suggested that racism may not be the only or the primary cause of racist outcomes in either of these areas of public service. It is necessary to look at the possible influence of an existing class ideology in the delivery of welfare services. As Peter Braham and Margaret Kiloh stress in Study Guide 3, we need to look beyond single political causes to wider economic factors if we are to understand the relationship between discourses and the extent to which black people are disadvantaged and discriminated against.

In examining the link that Solomos says was made between immigration and good community relations, for example, Braham and Kiloh suggest that you consider whether *uncontrolled* immigration could have provided a more favourable background to good community relations and to tackling racial disadvantage (Study Guide 3, p. 15). This is one way of problematizing this issue. It could, of course, have been problematized in another way. For example, one perspective you might like to consider is that the debate is not about whether immigration should be controlled or not, but about whether *skin colour* is a reason at all for controlling immigration. Why should skin colour have significance for community relations? What factors come together to give primacy to this question of colour? Does it make good economic sense to choose what appears to be an arbitrary marker such as skin colour for this purpose?

Responses to these questions may include the following points:

- Black people have for centuries been constructed as inferior and as a threat.

- This kind of construction came into being in order to justify exploitation and slavery and continues to the present day, changing its shape and form to accommodate the demands of different historical moments, but not changing its *basic* message.

- Skin colour as a marker of identity and exclusion has become so embedded in the various ideologies of white European thought and psyche that it has thus become a normal way of making sense of reality.

- Racist ideologies do not, therefore, need to exist for any single cause, such as serving capital, though they can and do serve this purpose. They are, however, only sustainable as long as groups continue to be racialized and there are differential power relations between 'racial groups', which in turn sustain the racist ideologies.

Activity 2

You may wish to remind yourself of other arguments which criticize the exclusive focus on 'race'. For example:

> ... it is not the prejudices of individual police officers, magistrates or judges which influence this application [of racist criteria] but the unthinking, unacknowledged routine assumptions and values of the legal system which lead to shared practice which discriminates against black people.
> (Study Guide 3, p. 77)

This statement suggests that, whatever the racism of individual police officers, it is merely symptomatic of wider problems within the legal system. What might this mean in terms of tackling the specific features of racism in the police force? Does this imply an overhaul of the legal system? Would policies be useful? Would such policies focus separately on racism or deal with all forms of inequality simultaneously? Might there be implications for the training of police officers? How might such training engage with the complexities of police racism outlined in Cohen's article in Reader 2?

Try not to spend more than ten minutes on this exercise. You are not expected to come up with all of the answers. The important thing is to attempt to grasp the nature and complexity of the issues. You might, for example, like to consider whether there could be short-term as well as long-term strategies for dealing with police racism.

If you would like to spend a little more time considering this issue, take a look at Activity 3. It provides a concrete example to help you think through the different elements of the debate.

Activity 3

In May 1992 a group of police officers in Los Angeles, USA, were found 'not guilty' of the excessive beating of a black man, despite the overwhelming evidence against them. In various discussions and reports about the causes of the subsequent riots which took place in a poor part of Los Angeles inhabited largely by black people, some commentators pointed to poverty as the main problem and others to the level of police harassment of black communities. In the light of this, take a few minutes to consider the following questions:

• What relationship might there be between poverty and disproportionately high levels of policing?

• Is there a relationship between class and levels of policing?

• Is it valid to draw comparisons between racism and policing in the USA and in Britain? Why?

To return to the basic issue of essentialism and reductionism, Knowles and Mercer (Reader 2) illustrated a different dimension to this debate. They argued that it is essentialist to suggest that the exclusion of black women's experiences from white feminist writing was an act of racism. They contend that it should be described as 'Eurocentrism', not racism, and that racism should be measured by its *material* effects. What material effects on black women might there be in their exclusion from white feminist literature? Might these be long-term as well as short-term effects? How adequate is it to measure racism *only* by its material effects? You may be interested to re-visit Brah's response to this question. You will find it on page 138 of Reader 2.

Here are two more questions, posed tentatively, for you to reflect upon. First, does the term 'Eurocentrism' accurately describe the exclusion of black people, bearing in mind that there have been black Europeans for many centuries and large numbers of black migrants and immigrants to Europe since World War 2? Is it another form of exclusion, or possibly a euphemism for racism? Second, what label might be applied to the exclusion (not necessarily intentional) of women from male accounts that purport to represent human beings in general?

Author's comment

There is a danger that in the effort to avoid essentialism and reductionism we could deny racism altogether. Whilst it is crucial that we are rigorously analytical in order to avoid reductionism, because it could obscure the complexities of human relations, it is also important that we do not exclude racism as a variable. Knowles and Mercer's definition of racism as those actions which have material effects is inadequate for reasons other than those proposed by Brah. Does it mean, for example, that a deliberately racist act of discrimination which nevertheless fails to produce the intended negative effect is not racist? In the discussion of ideology in Section 2.2 it was stated that racism was *routinized* into everyday social relations. Might it be possible that many of the 'normalized' expressions of racism go unrecognized precisely because they do not produce any visible effect? Are the subtleties, ambiguities, and assumptions which characterize the *everyday experiences* of racism to be ignored because their effects cannot be quantified? Might it be more useful to describe the 'racial' exclusion of black women as a form of 'weak' racism as suggested by Rattansi?

Our use of the term 'racist' to describe white individuals or groups needs to be more selective, not only because it is emotive, but also because we need to differentiate between those who live by and profess racist beliefs and those who reject them. The white feminists to which Knowles and Mercer referred were not racists in the sense that they deliberately set out to make black women invisible, but racism (and possibly class bias) may have been part of the process which informed the exclusion of black women from their frame of reference.

---

4   INSTITUTIONAL RACISM

4.1   Introduction

Two important ways in which racism is manifested are:

1   through *individual actions*; and
2   through the routine processes and procedures of *institutions*.

A detailed account of these concepts and of the policies and practices that derive from them can be found in Part 4 of Study Guide 3. The Resource Book contains many details of the different kinds of experiences and effects of racism faced by black people in their everyday lives.

Briefly, there are three ways in which the concept of institutional racism is discussed in ED356. The first examines the usefulness of the concept as an analytical tool; the second deals with the nature of institutional racism; and the third explores the effectiveness of institutional policies to counter racism. (I deal with the first and second of these below and devote the whole of Section 5 to the third.)

4.2   The concept of institutional racism

The concept of institutional racism is generally felt by contributors to the course to be a useful one for understanding the processes which discriminate and lead to group disadvantage.

The distinction is often made between *unintentional* and *intentional* racism, with the former more likely to be associated with norms and procedures of an institution and the latter with deliberate and vindictive actions by individuals. Individual racism and institutional racism are not, however, mutually exclusive. It is through individuals that the routine processes and procedures of institutions are carried out.

Institutional processes can be either directly or indirectly racist in their effects. An argument proposed by Jewson and Mason (Reader 3) is that those who draw up institutional policies often fail to engage with the complex nature of individuals and with the structural and ideological aspects of institutions.

4.3   The nature of institutional racism

In Study Guide 3 the suggestion was made that in a liberal democracy the concept of group disadvantage is barely recognized. Processes and procedures do not, therefore, have to be deliberately racist in order to discriminate against minority groups. Indeed, many practices which discriminate against black people were established long before they came to affect black communities. An example of this was provided in relation to housing allocation. It was suggested that a class ideology that led to house sizes being restricted in order to prevent working class people from having large families now discriminates against some Catholic and Asian families. The practice was not originally intended to operate against certain religious or ethnic groups. Another example related to the criminal justice system, where the 'colour-blind' approach to the selection of juries meant that black people could find themselves faced by all-white juries.

An example of the kind of tension that can occur between individual values, institutional processes and the effect of both on some groups was provided by Cecile Wright (Reader 1). She showed how teachers' values – the wish to treat children fairly and create equality of opportunity for all their pupils – conflicted with the routine processes in schools, such as dress codes for physical education. This disadvantaged particular groups of children, placing them in a difficult position with regard to their religious and cultural traditions. However, as you will by now have seen, the absence of intention in this case does not mean that there are no *deliberate* forms of racism within institutions. Many public as well as private institutions and organizations operate with criteria which deliberately exclude black people. You saw examples of this in the way that some estate agents and housing officials have excluded black clients from certain areas.

5   INSTITUTIONAL POLICY

5.1 Policy implementation and institutional racism

Is policy implementation the best way to deal with institutional racism? Perspectives differ. On the one hand, there is agreement that minority ethnic groups must be protected from unfair treatment, whether or not intended, and also from deliberate acts of racism. On the other hand, there is uncertainty about the effectiveness of attempts to achieve this by means of policies. There are those who view policies either as unworkable (Troyna and Hatcher, Reader 1), or counterproductive (Cohen, Reader 2), or not necessarily related to outcomes for disadvantaged groups (Gibbon, Reader 3). Troyna and Hatcher are sceptical of policies. In their view there is as yet no empirical evidence of their effectiveness. Cohen is concerned that antiracist policies could drive racism underground rather than counter it. Gibbon sees the *commitment* of an organization to equality rather than the policies themselves to be the only likely way to improve the position of minority ethnic groups.

Others believe that policy does have a role to play. Bagley (Reader 1) argues that, regardless of individual commitment, the obligation to comply with policy should be non-negotiable. How does this fit in with Cohen's view that racism could be driven underground? Bagley contends that the content of the policy would need to be collectively discussed and negotiated. However, the process of discussion and negotiation would have to be so conducted that participants contributed equally to the policy rather than felt that they were its targets. For Ouseley (Reader 1), some of the gains made by black people in local situations could not have happened without equal opportunities policies.

Ben Tovim *et al.* are of the view that policies can help to bring about reform within local authorities, but this requires not only persistence on the part of those with a commitment to the issue, but also an understanding of the formal and informal structures of power within these organizations. This view is supported by Richardson (Reader 1), whose account of policy development in two local education authorities underlines the importance of awareness of the different forces that act to undermine attempts to implement policies aimed at achieving racial equality. In this respect, you may recall Richardson's discussion of the part played by the media, which is supported by the accounts in Study Guide 1 and the article by Ouseley (Reader 1).

5.2   Contexts and types of policy

The above differences of perspective appear to be largely dependent
on the context within which the policy is implemented and the
particular type of policy being discussed. The context could vary from
large organizations such as a local authority or the police force to
smaller organizations such as a school or a youth club. There are
basically two types of policy under discussion:

1   policies to deal with racist harassment. (I use 'racist' here for the
    reason given in Study Guide 1, p. 56);
2   policies to promote equality of opportunity.

These are not necessarily mutually exclusive: an equal opportunities
policy generally covers racist harassment. But a school, for example,
might have a policy on multicultural education which is intended to
cover equality of opportunity and another to deal specifically with
racist harassment.

In housing, where the local authority is involved, and where there
may be a conflict between black people themselves wishing to take an
active part in dealing with problems of racist harassment and local
officials intent on maintaining control, it is not so easy to determine
whose interests are best served by the implementation of a policy (see
Ginsburg, Reader 3).

5.3   The efficacy of policies

In Reader 1, Ouseley documents some local policy successes in the
area of employment, though, like Ginsburg, he underlines the
importance of government support, resources and commitment.
Gibbon (Reader 3) showed that, in any organization, policies for
achieving equality of opportunity were not likely to succeed if
commitment was absent. Even where such policies were accepted as
'a good thing', they were not necessarily at the top of the
organization's priorities.

Cohen's concern (Reader 2) emerges from his close study of the factors
which determine racist behaviour, particularly amongst young, white,
working class people. In his view, policies to tackle racism would be
resisted by young white people who may already be in conflict with
authority and who view *themselves,* and not black people, as the
'underdogs'. To criminalize racist harassment through antiracist
policies would, in his view, be counter-productive.

Author's comment

You may feel general sympathy with the arguments of Cohen, who is acutely aware of the complex workings of racist youth cultures. You may, however, also want to consider other aspects of this issue.

1   Racist harassment causes untold misery, fear and even death, as you saw from the evidence in *'Race' in Britain Today*. What is to be done for families who are racially harassed if such criminal acts are not dealt with in the same way as all criminal acts?

2   Cohen suggests that there should be 'appropriate sanctions' to deal with racist harassment in order to avoid the 'harsh "super egoism" associated with doctrinaire antiracism' (Reader 2, p. 97). Is it not possible that there would always be conflict over what constitutes 'appropriate sanctions' for dealing with racist intimidation, and that such sanctions are likely to be labelled 'doctrinaire' (however appropriate they may be) by those who are opposed to the use of any form of sanction?

Troyna and Hatcher's analysis (Reader 1) comes from their work with primary school children. Like Cohen, they recommend close engagement with the cultures of young children in order to devise appropriate methods of countering children's racism.

Bagley (Reader 1) is concerned less with children's racism than with the important role that teachers play in influencing and educating children. A viable school policy would be one that addressed teacher racism. In his view a proper sense of ownership of a policy would obviate the assumption that a policy is there to police and undermine teachers' professionalism. It would exist as a guidance document to assist staff in recognizing racism in order to enable them to implement a multicultural curriculum.

Activity 4

It is worth pausing here for a minute to take a critical look at the idea of 'ownership'. Does it assume the absence of hierarchical structures within organizations? Would all the members of staff of a school, for instance, have an equal say in the form, content and implementation of a policy? What were the obstacles to arriving at a consensus amongst the teachers in Bagley's study (see Reader 1, pp. 237– 43)?

---

6 EQUAL OPPORTUNITIES POLICIES

6.1 *Introduction*

The pursuit of equality of opportunity has been an increasingly popular strategy for antiracists and feminists. The concept of equal opportunities is, however, neither straightforward nor self-evident. Jewson and Mason (Reader 3) showed how the discourse of equality of opportunity shifts according to context and to ideological or theoretical perspective. Focusing on employment, they distinguish between a liberal approach to equality of opportunity, where the stress is on processes and assumes equal starting points, and a radical approach, where the stress is on equal *outcomes.*

These distinctions, according to Jewson and Mason, serve to underline some of the practical tensions and conceptual confusions that beset equal opportunities policies. The problem of implementing such policies is, however, more complex than a focus on conceptual confusion implies. Ben Tovim *et al.* (Reader 3) discuss how equal opportunities policies can become a mechanism for marginalizing and disenfranchizing groups, as well as being vulnerable to manipulation by local political representatives. Ouseley (Reader 1) outlined the extent to which such policies could become victims of media hostility, bureaucratic inefficiency and lack of commitment on the part of central government and of local authority officials. The radical policies which he discusses were specifically aimed at tackling racial discrimination, so that it was the mechanisms of subjective and institutional racism that operated to exclude black people from employment which were the focus of antiracist campaigns and strategies, and which stimulated other strategic campaigns against inequality. He contends that 'for race equality programmes to be meaningful, they require an independent existence within a framework of an equal opportunities policy' (Reader 1, p. 127).

How does this differ from the perspective offered by Gilroy (Reader 2)? Racism, according to Gilroy, is at the very core of politics. For Gilroy, equal opportunities can provide little more than 'a coat of paint' to the problems of inequality. He is also critical of antiracist activism. Some antiracist activists, he asserts, are able to sustain their struggles 'independently of the lives, dreams and aspirations of the majority of blacks from whose experience they derive their authority to speak' (Reader 2, p. 51).

How does this fit in with Ouseley's account of improved employment prospects for black people in Hackney which were struggled for by antiracist 'professionals' working with grassroot communities? Ouseley gives an indication of the range of forces which come into conflict over the issue of 'race'. He also points out both the strengths and the weaknesses of the antiracist struggle in a local context. You might also like to compare Gilroy's statement (quoted above) with Ben Tovim *et al.*, for whom local authorities are 'sites of struggle'. For them, the outcome of struggles between competing ideologies in an arena marked by tension, contradiction and conflict *cannot be predicted*. It is therefore difficult, in their view, to establish the 'correct' form of campaign. But they also stress that:

> Reforms and policy initiatives which result in part from these struggles over conditions help define future conditions of struggle. For this reason alone, planned struggle cannot afford to ignore or to dismiss as divisive or gestural reforms, such as equal opportunity policies, specialist race staff, new committees and units, and monitoring; instead it must acknowledge them as integral parts of the conditions of struggle.

(Reader 3, p. 216)

Television

The round-table discussion in TV8, *Beyond the Debates*, addresses, amongst other topics, the issue of antiracism as a strategy.

6.2   Theoretical differences

What theoretical differences might there be between the perspectives outlined above? They all begin with the premise that there is social disadvantage. Ouseley (Reader 1) focuses on a specific type of disadvantage, that caused by *racial* discrimination in employment, and takes as his starting point the practical elements of such discrimination. Hence, for him, the problem is not so much that antiracists focus on racism and racial discrimination to the exclusion of other issues, but that those who control and allocate resources operate in ways which divide disadvantaged groups. He would, therefore, contend that unless racism is given a specific focus it will be marginalized. He also points to the way in which antiracist struggles in the former Greater London Council served as a catalyst for other groups seeking to tackle disadvantage, or opened up the issue of inequality generally. Ben Tovim *et al.* (Reader 3) take a similar view, stressing the tendency for local officials and politicians to marginalize issues relating to inequality. What does Gilroy (Reader 2) suggest might counter this tendency?

Gilroy argues that we turn our backs on the 'state' and establish broad alliances which cut across national and cultural boundaries. The difficulty with this, an antiracist might reply, is that it does not address the day-to-day problems of people facing *racial* discrimination. What practical steps could be taken to prevent discriminatory practices? Equal opportunities policies in Hackney may have been no more than 'a coat of paint' in relation to the pervasive nature of racism, but in real terms that 'coat of paint' meant jobs and improved life chances where these might otherwise not have been available. Whilst the shift in the discourse of 'race' from biological to cultural factors needs to be recognized and understood, we also need to harness this understanding to local grassroot struggles.

Activity 5

You might like to construct an imaginary discussion between Ouseley and Gilroy in a style similar to that between Knowles and Mercer and Brah in Study Guide 2 (pp. 25–6). Some questions that might be asked are:

- How might 'the democratic movement of civil society' overcome the competing demands and different priorities of its members?

- As we cannot wish the *specific* features of racism away, how are problems of the marginalization of black peoples to be avoided in this broad movement?

- How is the question of differential access to power to be addressed?

In responding to Activity 5, you may have considered Gilroy's suggestion to be an attempt to move away from binary divisions of black and white and establish a political movement which takes diversity and difference as its starting point. We will look at this issue in Section 9.2.

6.3 The efficacy of equal opportunities policies

Despite differences of theoretical perspective and of emphasis, the various contributors seem united in regarding the link between equal opportunities policies, implementation and outcomes as a tenuous one. There is also broad agreement that one of the major reasons for this is the absence of commitment on the part of central government and 'the state', embodied in public organizations and institutions. It might be argued that it is precisely this lack of commitment that makes equal opportunities policies necessary as a means for local groups to tackle discrimination. There is, however, broad agreement amongst contributors to this course that to attempt to tackle racism in isolation from other forms of social inequality will be neither sufficient nor successful.

7   THE EDUCATION DEBATE

7.1   Introduction

The education debate takes us into an area where differences of
strategy are most marked. Governments have often assumed that
education is one of the main means of tackling both the level of
disadvantage suffered by young black people and the 'prejudices' of
white society. You will be familiar with the reasons for the setting up
of the Rampton and Swann Committees (see Course Introduction, pp.
21–6 and Study Guide 1, pp. 30–2). Briefly, both reports focused
attention on the dissatisfaction of black communities with the
education of their children and the 'underachievement' of black
children in school. (You heard some of the concerns voiced by black
people in the discussion on Audio-cassette 2 about supplementary
schooling.) The question of 'black underachievement' and of racism in
the education system was placed on the educational and political
agenda. But why was education seen to be so important in tackling
the problems that black people faced and preventing the sorts of
disturbances that had spilled out onto the streets of British cities
during the first half of the 1980s?

You may recall what was said about this in the Course Introduction.
'Race' and education were described as 'an explosive mixture'. Now
that you have studied ED356, how do you view the notion that
education plays an important role in the ideological definitions of
national culture? In this context, what role might education play in a
culturally diverse society? What is understood by cultural diversity?

7.2   The concept of cultural diversity

Different understandings of culture

Rattansi suggested in the Course Introduction that the term *diversity*
was probably the most accurate for describing the nature of British
society.

Activity 6

What do you understand by diversity in the British context? Write down the features which you think make Britain a diverse society.

You may have concluded that diversity describes a society which has within it peoples of different backgrounds, cultures, ethnicities, religions, languages and so forth. This clearly entails a complex understanding of the rights and expectations of the different groups that make up that society as well as obligations that they all carry. But this kind of diversity implies different things to different people. Central to these perspectives are different conceptualizations of culture, where culture is either taken to be a static phenomenon or a dynamic process which is subject to continuous redefinition. Some of these perspectives are outlined briefly here.

From the political Right, Britain is characterized as a monocultural society and diversity is seen as a threat to the perceived 'unity' of the nation. It is argued by many proponents of this view that it is not only right, but the absolute duty of minority ethnic groups to assimilate into the 'mainstream' culture, 'mainstream' being seen as more or less synonymous with 'English'. Boundaries of belonging and 'Otherness' are drawn along 'racial' lines. Black peoples and black peoples' cultures have been constructed not only as alien and therefore 'outside' the national culture, but also as *incapable of belonging* to it. The assumption is that culture is static, liable to contamination, and grounded in biology.

Despite the emphasis on pluralism, the liberal democratic view of diversity exemplified by the Swann Report differs little, it would seem, from that of the Right in its assumptions of culture as something static and grounded in biology. The multiculturalist strategies to which this led encouraged the celebration of 'fixed' cultures and emphasized tolerance and acceptance of 'Others'. It is possible to read into this perspective a vision of an undifferentiated majority culture, thereby placing minority ethnic groups on the periphery of national life. Paul Gilroy (Reader 2) used the term 'ethnic absolutism' to describe the tendency to define culturally different groups as being internally homogeneous. He was of the view that this contributed to the marginalization of black people. This view of ethnicity, according to Gilroy and Yuval-Davis (Reader 2), was promoted by multiculturalists and antiracists, without clear analysis of the separatist and 'fundamentalist' tendencies which it encouraged. Such educational strategies, Yuval-Davis argues, encouraged the racialization of religion, thus obscuring class and gender differences and conflicts within religious movements.

Another view of culture is exemplified in the work of the black writers, artists and film-makers that you saw in TV5 and TV6, *The Burden of Representation*. They reject having 'ethnic' identities imposed on them and on their work and challenge the notion of *unified* and stable collective identities. Drawing on a range of experiences and histories in naming their identities, they develop the idea of culture as multi-dimensional and as a process of 'self-naming'. Stuart Hall's article on 'New ethnicities' (Reader 2) reinforces this view that culture is not fixed, but is constructed and therefore subject to change in and through different historical and social processes.

Modood (Reader 2) emphasizes a different aspect of culture in his discussion of British Muslims. Whilst not dissenting from the view that cultural identities are discursive and political constructs, he argues that there are historical processes (the historical tensions between Christians and Muslims, for example), as well as contemporary events (such as the Salman Rushdie affair), which lead to people's need for a sense of community identity. What problem does Yuval-Davis identify in this perspective of 'community'? This is discussed in Section 9.1 on 'race' and gender.

But, first, it is worth re-visiting the contending perspectives on the 'underachievement' of black children in order to look at the kinds of strategies to which these different understandings of culture gave rise.

7.3   The 'underachievement' debate

During the 1980s two main explanations were proposed for the 'underachievement' of black children. These were (1) black children's low self-esteem and (2) teacher racism. In very simple terms, multicultural education was a response to the first 'problem'. Black children would be taught about their own cultures and, at the same time, white children would learn about and become tolerant of 'other' cultures. The problem of 'underachievement' was, from this perspective, projected onto black children themselves, whilst racism was defined as something that was lodged in the prejudiced minds of individuals. However, a study carried out by Maureen Stone refuted the idea that black children suffered from low self-esteem and, indeed, the idea that school was the best place for children to be taught about their own family cultures (Stone, 1981).

Antiracist education was the response to the second of the explanations for black pupils' 'underachievement' – that of teacher racism. Studies pointed to the differential treatment of black – in particular Afro-Caribbean – children in schools, and teacher racism became the focus of antiracist strategy. The problem, it was argued, was that, as Britain was a racist society, the institutions were also racist and it was therefore inevitable that white teachers, who were part of the dominant culture, would be racist. You are already familiar with the critique of this perspective as being both essentialist (white teachers are necessarily racist because they are white) and reductionist (black children's 'problems' are caused by racism alone). This is, of course, a very schematic account. There are overlaps between the multicultural and antiracist perspectives, particularly at the level of classroom practice.

Officially, as Troyna (Reader 1) pointed out, the assumptions of local education authorities mirrored the assimilationist assumptions of central government. There was little commitment to addressing the concerns that black communities were themselves identifying. The debate about 'underachievement', Rattansi (Reader 2) argues, is itself more complex than the two perspectives outlined here suggest. A question generally absent from the debate is that of class. Within the different categories of South Asian pupils, some achieve consistently better than others. Pupils of Indian background, for example, achieve better as a group than pupils of Bangladeshi origin as a group. More recently, the question being posed is whether working-class pupils of Afro-Caribbean origin achieve any less than working-class white pupils, and whether gender is a factor (see Resource Book, Section 10).

8 OTHER STRATEGIES TO COUNTER RACISM

8.1 Racism awareness training

The conceptualization of racism as something lodged in the prejudiced minds of individuals led to a particular type of antiracist strategy – racism awareness training (RAT). Taking its cue from the awareness-raising programmes which began in the United States, RAT was seen as the way to deal with the problem of racism, not only in schools but in all other areas where black people met with discrimination and prejudice. This method of 'training' was roundly condemned by many antiracists for being guilt-inducing and therefore counter-productive. The RAT approach risked alienating and disempowering antiracist white people by its assumption that white people as such were racist. As you saw from Ouseley's article in Reader 1, it was, therefore, an easy target for the populist press. Another criticism was that this kind of analysis and the strategies to which it gave rise focused exclusively on racism at the expense of other experiences such as gender, class and sexuality. You studied the critique of this method of antiracism in connection with Stuart Hall's discussion with James Donald on Audio-cassette 1 and in the articles in Part 1 of Block 2.

8.2 Antiracist education

By the mid-1980s antiracists had begun to re-evaluate these educational strategies, and whilst remnants of the earlier more doctrinaire methods still remained in some areas, strategies were shifting from RAT to antiracist education (ARE). This fact was not always acknowledged by the media who, intent on 'demonizing' any programmes which focused on racial equality, overlooked the positive gains and focused on sensationalizing the few examples of conflict (see Richardson and Ouseley, Reader 1).

The context within which antiracist education was implemented could not guarantee either immediate or obvious 'success'. 'Success' is, of course, a highly subjective concept in that a great deal depends on the criteria one uses for judging success or failure. Without official endorsement and resourcing, struggles for equality and for equality of opportunity are likely to be continuing *struggles*, as Ouseley and Richardson (Reader 1) and Ben Tovim *et al.* (Reader 3) show.

Ouseley and Ben Tovim *et al.* in particular stress the role of official bureaucratic processes in undermining such struggles. Troyna indicated in his article how *official* debates were underpinned by an assimilationist ideology, regardless of whether policies were labelled multicultural or antiracist. Discourses were racialized or deracialized depending on the political perspectives, the intentions, or the level of understanding of the politics of 'race' of those involved in official policy and practice. (This was not confined to education, as is demonstrated by Dominelli's discussion of the social services in Reader 3.)

Antiracist educators, aware of the problems of the racism awareness training of the early 1980s and attempting to build a broader-based antiracist politics, were no less likely than others working in the area of equality of opportunity to be isolated and under-funded. Guy and Menter and Ouseley (Reader 1) underlined the importance of funding and of the control of funding in progressing projects for 'racial' equality and equality of opportunity. Hardy and Vieler-Porter (Reader 1) pointed to government policies in education which in their view are hostile to an egalitarian politics. Were these processes a product of the barrenness of antiracist analysis, or an example of the shifting nature of ideologies and political priorities? What were some of the weaknesses of antiracist strategies?

8.3   The critique of antiracism

You may recall the critique of antiracism mounted in Part 1 of Reader 2. Antiracists were criticized for being essentialist and reductionist. How well is this borne out in articles by antiracist contributors to Reader 1?

Cecile Wright, for example, exposed profound contradictions in the values of white teachers and the outcomes of their relations with their black pupils. Teachers were said to be caring and committed to equality of opportunity. Furthermore, Asian children satisfied teacher stereotypes of the 'ideal' pupil: 'industrious and hard-working'. Yet teachers not only succeeded in humiliating some of the Asian pupils, they also unintentionally encouraged racism amongst the white pupils. There is also evidence of the extent to which teachers' relations with Afro-Caribbean children, in particular boys and Rastafarians, could be prejudicial to the interests of these children. Afro-Caribbean children were said to have the same attitude to education as white children, yet they received a disproportionate amount of criticism and were sometimes selectively punished for offences in which white pupils were also involved (see also Gillborn, 1988). How can we explain this?

Activity 7

Why does there appear to be such a strong need to control Afro-Caribbean children, especially boys, even from such an early age?

Could Rattansi's discussion of sexuality and the psychoanalytic approach discussed by Pajaczkowska and Young in Reader 2 help us to understand this? Have the negative images and representations of black (and in particular African) people over the centuries become so normalized that teachers who *care* about their pupils nevertheless function with stereotypes of them? What role might contemporary representations of black people play in reinforcing and reproducing these stereotypes? What role might class play?

Take a few minutes to reflect on these questions. If necessary, go back to the articles by Rattansi and by Pajaczkowska and Young to remind yourself of their arguments.

How do the other writers in Reader 1 stand up to the charge of essentialism and reductionism? Bagley discussed the contradictory tendencies of teachers who viewed pupils from minority ethnic groups as 'outsiders' whilst simultaneously pronouncing their professional integrity in relation to all their pupils. How might one avoid an essentialist view of the teachers' actions?

Mac an Ghaill talked of the multi-dimensionality of black pupils' experiences, thus showing that, although racism was a significant factor in the experiences of the black students, it was not the *only* influence in their lives. Troyna and Hatcher, too, referred to the need for a broader understanding and analysis of racist incidents which did not separate them off from factors of social class, gender and youth cultures.

At the classroom level, antiracist strategies varied widely, as you saw from the different approaches used by the teachers in the studies by Burgess-Macey and Short and Carrington (Reader 1). In other words, there is no single, monolithic antiracist strategy. They all recognize racism as a problem, that is what makes them antiracists, but they also recognize that it is neither a simple phenomenon, nor the only phenomenon. To whom then does the critique of antiracism in Block 2 refer?

The contributors discussed above illustrate the way in which antiracist strategies have shifted from the assumptions of RAT. Might it be the RAT strategy at which the critique is largely aimed? Unfortunately, this is not clear. Many antiracists working in education, in particular teachers, remain conscious of contradictions in their work and in their pupils' perceptions of 'race'. But to what extent do they harness this knowledge to the strategies they employ? In Study Guide 1 it was pointed out that antiracist strategies which attempt to tackle racism at an individual as well as an institutional level have differed not just from region to region, but often from school to school. Classroom strategies are, of course, never simple, as those of you who are teachers will know. 'Success' cannot be guaranteed precisely because one is dealing with a variety of complex individuals in a complex setting.

The discussion of TV4, *Empires of the Mind*, in Study Guide 2 (pp. 46–8) may have given you some insight into the difficulties the question of 'race', in particular, poses for teachers. If we consider teaching to be a developmental process, is it useful to castigate teachers, as Rattansi does in Reader 2, for not using strategies which have played no part in their own education? In the light of the theoretical contributions of discourse analysis to our understanding of racism, and Rattansi's contention that 'racism and ethnocentrism are not necessarily confined to white groups' (p. 36), what practical strategies might be devised for teaching about 'race' in schools? And how is the relationship between racism and sexuality (Rattansi; Pajaczkowska and Young, Reader 2) to be incorporated into educational strategy given the kind of resistance from teachers described by Bagley in Reader 1? These are difficult questions. They form part of the ongoing debate in which this course has sought to engage you. The difficulties involved in relating theory to practice are exemplified in the debate about positive and negative images discussed in Block 2.

8.4   Positive/negative images

The perspective on cultural identity as a process of self-naming, which we discussed earlier, includes a critique of the kinds of strategies which have been employed to counter negative representations of black people. You may have had difficulty getting to grips with the main elements of this debate about positive images and negative images. The important point being made by Hall in Reader 2, and by the artists and film-makers in TV5 and TV6, *The Burden of Representation*, is that it is politically ineffective to replace negative images of culture and identity with positive images by mimicking the same dominant framework of culture and identity. What these artists have done is to position themselves outside these modes of representation, problematizing the question of identity and politicizing the forms of representation. Lola Young expresses this in her discussion of Toni Morrison's novel *Beloved*.

> The quest is for a personal and collective identity based on self-esteem which can survive in a racist society, for the expression of a specific 'Black consciousness' and *for a way of expressing oral and cultural traditions in a language which escapes the entrapment of dominant discourses* ... Black authors, having identified the oppressors' language for what it is – the imagination of the dominant culture embodied in words – use, control and expand the vocabulary to create something that speaks to the experiences of Black communities. *In so doing, they combat white people's lack of perception of Blacks as individuated beings.*
>
> (Reader 2, p. 212, *my emphasis*)

Author's comment

You may consider that this perspective does indeed offer a more progressive strategy, moving, as it does, away from absolutist and binary oppositions of black culture/white culture. You may, however, also want to reflect on what it actually means in the daily interface with racism experienced by black people in Britain which is so clearly documented in *'Race' in Britain Today*. Does it offer a coherent political lead? Is this but *one* strategy made possible by the specific, and to some extent autonomous, medium within which artists, writers and film-makers work? What does it mean to a teacher, for example, faced with negative stereotypes of black people in the books and teaching materials in the school? How can a teacher foster a positive sense of identity in black pupils when racist images and representations permeate the world views of British children through a myriad of forms? S/he can, of course, problematize the meaning of identity. But is this enough? Might it be possible to build an antiracist politics which both rejects dominant discourses and also engages with the differential power relations implied by such discourses?

Audio-cassette

This would be a good point at which to listen to Audio-cassette 4, Side 1. My discussion with Stuart Hall lasts for about 30 minutes.

---

9 IDENTITY AND FORMS OF MOBILIZATION

9.1 'Race' and gender

The importance of identity in debates about gender and in questions of religious affiliation was raised in Section 7.2. Of importance in discussions about identity, as in any other 'race'-related discussions about policy and practice, is the sensitive issue of who speaks for whom and on what terms. To what extent do discussions which underline the importance of culture to an understanding of the dynamics of 'race' also acknowledge the importance of gender and other forms of inequality? Yuval-Davis, for example, is sceptical of fundamentalist demands for separate schools, whose purpose, in her view, is 'to bring up girls to be dutiful wives and mothers' (Reader 2, p. 286). One of the criticisms made of multicultural and antiracist education has been that the tendency to focus exclusively on single issues has led people to overlook the importance of gender relations within religious organizations and consequently to collude with the oppression of women. 'The categorization of minority communities in primarily religious terms assumes them to be internally unified, homogeneous entities with no class or gender differences or conflicts' (Reader 2, p. 284).

Brah (Reader 2) takes the debate about who speaks for whom into the arena of black and white feminist politics. Disagreeing with Knowles and Mercer (Reader 2) in their construction of separate black and white feminisms as essentialist, she suggests instead that 'they represent struggles over political frameworks for analysis; the meanings of theoretical concepts; the relationship between theory, practice and subjective experiences; and over political priorities and modes of mobilizations' (Reader 2, p. 138). Mama (Reader 3) supports Brah, agreeing with her that the colonial experience which African, Caribbean and South Asian women share gives them a basis on which to organize together without stifling different cultural experiences.

However, whilst Mama and Brah agree on the effects of racism, they differ in their explanations of the causal relations between racism and the differential position of black women. Mama is of the view that black women are exploited by the 'state' for the sake of capital, whilst Brah sees racism as diffuse and not related to a single cause. They are, however, both concerned about the role of the state in fostering 'patriarchal racism' and the way that particular stereotypical constructions of different groups of black women position them *differentially* within the social structure. Stereotypes of black women go a long way back into the history of racism, as evidenced by Sander Gilman's account of constructions of black women's sexuality (Reader 2). They are produced and reproduced historically (see Pajaczkowska's account of the entertainment industry in Reader 2) and, according to Brah and Mama, inform the way that black women are positioned within different institutions of the state.

The question of how women mobilize against discrimination and disadvantage is an issue of considerable debate and relates to wider debates about how black people in general mobilize.

Audio-cassette

Listen now to Audio-cassette 4, Side 2, where Avtar Brah and I discuss some of the debates within feminism. The discussion lasts about 30 minutes.

9.2 Contestation around the term 'black'

The relationship between culture and different forms of mobilization is complex. The term 'black' has entered the debates about culture in a specific way in Britain. What arguments have been posed against its use as an organizing and unifying principle?

Activity 8

Make a note of all the arguments you can remember *against* the use of the term 'black' as a political symbol or conceptual tool. Try not to spend more than 10 minutes on this exercise.

Comment

Some commentators argue that:
- 'Black' referred specifically to the historical experience of people of sub-Saharan African descent.
- The concept can incorporate Asians in a political sense only and it therefore denies Asian cultural identity.

- The concept is meaningless to many South Asians who do not define themselves as 'black'.

- It serves to conceal the cultural needs of groups other than those of African-Caribbean origin.

A response to the above points was outlined by Brah (Reader 2). She argues that:

> the term 'black' does not have to be construed in essentialist terms. It can have different political and cultural meanings in different contexts ... [In] post-war Britain ... the concrete political struggles in which the new meaning was grounded acknowledged cultural differences but sought to accomplish political unity against racism. In any case, the issue of cultural difference cannot be posed purely in terms of differences between South Asian and African-Caribbean cultures. There are, for example, many differences between African and Caribbean cultures ...

> ... South Asians will frequently describe themselves as 'kale' (black) when discussing issues of racism ... As a social movement, black activism has aimed to generate solidarity; it has not necessarily assumed that all members of the diverse black communities inevitably identify with the concept in its British usage ...

> (Reader 2, pp. 128–9)

With regard to the argument that the term 'black' serves to conceal cultural needs of groups other than those of African-Caribbean origin, Brah states that:

> This particular critique is steeped in 'ethnicism' [which] posits 'ethnic difference' as the primary modality around which social life is constituted and experienced [and] ... seeks to impose stereotypic notions of 'common cultural need' upon heterogeneous groups with diverse social aspirations and interests.

> (ibid., p. 129)

Another argument against the use of 'black' is that it excludes white minority groups who also experience racism. What might Brah's response be? What is your own response?

What difficulties does Gilroy (Reader 2) identify with this form of mobilization? Gilroy's concern centres on the effects of what he termed 'ethnic absolutism' to describe the dangers of groups viewing themselves from within their own particular ethnic grouping. This, according to Gilroy, is the very same strategy which enables the political Right to construct an image of a single unified white culture, and to construct antiracism as 'loony' and demonic. It seems that what Gilroy is saying is that this could be avoided if we were to take notions of 'difference' and of diversity as our starting point for building broad social alliances. Is he making a similar point to that made by Knowles and Mercer in their account of black and white feminisms (Reader 2)?

If you recall, Knowles and Mercer were of the view that the creation of a separate constituency of black women was not intended to tackle the question of gender inequality, but to determine the qualification for inclusion into that constituency. Gilroy and Cohen (Reader 2) make a similar point when they assert that antiracist activists exploit ethnicity for 'cultural capital'. The critique seems to be about the *motives* of black women and of antiracists. Are their arguments convincing?

How does this fit in with the accounts about Brent and Berkshire LEA provided by Richardson in Reader 1? Might it be argued that the above critics overlook the point that Brah made in Reader 2, that it is not only how individuals *view themselves*, but how they are *positioned* in a hierarchically structured society, that needs to be taken into account.

If you recall, Richardson described how, in Berkshire, *different* constituencies led by the white middle-class worked *collectively* against the threat posed to the LEA's multicultural policy, and succeeded. In Brent, it was not the existence of different constituencies as such which made them targets of attack, but the hostility of the Conservative government and the media to changes which were the initiative of black and working-class people.

10   Taking stock

The issues you have dealt with in this course are not only difficult but contentious. The main point is that we should not only know or 'prove' there is racism, but also understand how and why this is so. In order to understand, we need models of social theory which take account of the complex and contradictory nature of social relations. This has been the central thrust of the criticism of essentialism and reductionism. The question of strategy remains one to be constantly reviewed and re-evaluated. The effectiveness of particular strategies, it seems clear, cannot be predicted. The contexts in which strategy is applied are themselves diffuse and complex.

A pressing question that needs to be addressed has to do with developing strategies which are appropriate for contemporary Britain in all its diversity. What programmes and political agendas can be devised which give voice to the interests and concerns of British-born generations of black people whose experiences of racism may differ in some respects from those of their parents and grandparents? Despite some of the differences of experience, British-born black people are still not considered 'British'. The debate about 'new ethnicities' indicates that within black cultural politics there is a movement away from 'race' relations to human relations and to notions of 'difference' as the central concern. Such a politics presents us with a serious challenge to be encouraged, not discouraged, by the need to learn to communicate effectively across our differences, and to be alert to the hierarchical and dominative relations within which such dialogue takes place. If a politics of difference is capable of informing grassroot struggles and challenging and ultimately transforming those forces which seek to homogenize and to position groups differentially in society, we will indeed be moving a long way beyond the debates.

References

GILLBORN, D. (1990) *'Race' Ethnicity and Education: teaching and learning in multi-ethnic schools*, London, Unwin Hyman.

STONE, M. (1981) *The Education of the Black Child: the myth of multiracial education,* London, Fontana.